MARS

Robin Kerrod

Lerner Publications Company • Minneapolis

This edition published in 2000

Lerner Publications Company
A division of Lerner Publishing Group
241 First Avenue North, Minneapolis MN 55401

Website address: www.lernerbooks.com

© 2000 by Graham Beehag Books

Library of Congress Cataloging-in-Publication Data

Kerrod, Robin
    Mars / Robin Kerrod.
       p. cm. – (Planet library)
    Includes index.
    Summary: Introduces the planet Mars, with information about its atmosphere, surface features, and exploration by NASA spacecraft.
    ISBN 0-8225-3906-3 (lib. bdg.)
Mars (Planet) – Juvenile literature. [1. Mars (Planet)]
I. Title. II Series: Kerrod, Robin. Planet library
QB641.K23   2000
523.43—dc21   99-31617

Printed in Singapore by Star Standard Industries [PTE] Ltd
Bound in the United States of America
2 3 4 5 6 7 – OS – 07 06 05 04 03 02

CONTENTS

Introducing Mars

Mars looks like a bright reddish-orange light in our night sky. The planet's unique color reminded ancient peoples of fire and blood. The Romans named the planet after Mars, their god of war. Because of its distinct color, Mars is often called the Red Planet.

Mars is the fourth planet in the solar system, going out from the Sun. That makes it one of our closest neighbors. Mars, along with Mercury, Venus, and Earth, is one of the four terrestrial planets. Terrestrial means Earth-like. The terrestrial planets are all made up of rocky layers surrounding a metal core. Mars also has an atmosphere, or layer of gases, surrounding it. Beneath the atmosphere, ice caps rise at the chilly north and south poles.

A close-up view of the Red Planet, Mars

Mars's surface has many Earth-like features, including volcanoes, deep valleys, and what appear to be dried-out riverbeds.

Many people once thought that life, even intelligent life, might exist on Mars. But information and pictures from space probes have not shown that life exists on the Red Planet. Conditions on the surface are so harsh that life could not survive. There is no liquid water, the temperatures are too cold, and the atmosphere does not contain enough of the gases needed to support life.

However, long ago, Mars was probably much warmer, had a thicker atmosphere, and had flowing water. Astronomers (scientists who study outer space) continue to search for evidence that some form of life did grow on Mars many years ago. Perhaps, as we learn more about our mysterious neighbor, we will find proof that life once existed on the Red Planet.

Mars Basics

Mars is one of the smallest planets in the solar system and one of the closest to Earth. It is easy to spot when it shines brightly in our night sky.

As the fourth planet in the solar system, Mars lies in between Earth and Jupiter. Mars's distance from the Sun varies, from about 128 to 155 million miles (206–250 million km). At that distance, it takes longer to orbit, or circle, the Sun than Earth does. Mars completes one orbit in 687 Earth-days—nearly two Earth-years.

CLOSE ENCOUNTERS

Mars has a diameter, or distance across, of about 4,220 miles (6,800 km). That's just over half the diameter of Earth. Only Mercury and Pluto are smaller. Despite its small size, Mars is an easy planet to spot in our night sky because of its reddish color.

Above: Mars is small compared with our own planet. It could fit inside Earth nearly seven times.

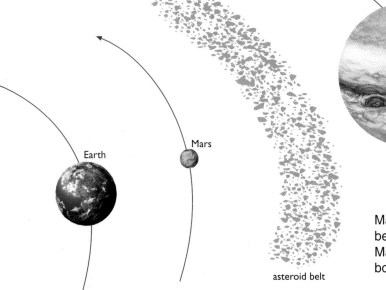

Earth

Mars

asteroid belt

Jupiter

Mars is located in the solar system between Earth and Jupiter. Between Mars and Jupiter is the ring of rocky bodies we call the asteroids.

But Mars is not easily visible all the time. It shines most brightly when Mars and Earth move close together as they travel in their orbits around the Sun. The two planets come closest to each other about every 26 months. Sometimes Mars and Earth come within 35 million miles (56 million km) of each other during these close encounters. Only Venus travels closer to Earth.

THROUGH A TELESCOPE

If you looked at Mars through a telescope, you would notice dark and bright areas on its surface. The bright parts are covered by dust, sand, and rocks. They make up about two-thirds of the planet's surface. The dark areas cover about one-third of the planet. Mars's dark parts are often called maria, or seas, although they do not contain water. From Earth, they appear to change in size and position over time. These changes could be caused by sand that blows across Mars and covers up some of the dark areas.

Telescopes also reveal another prominent feature on Mars—white caps at its north and south poles. Like the caps at Earth's poles, Mars's polar caps are made up of frozen ice. The size and appearance of Mars's ice caps changes throughout the year.

MARS'S MAKEUP

Like Earth, Mars is made up of several rocky layers. Its thick crust, or hard outer layer, is about 125 miles (220 km) deep. The crust covers a deeper layer of heavier rock called the mantle, which is about 1,360 miles (2,190 km) thick. At Mars's center is a core made up mainly of iron. Unlike Earth's liquid metal core, Mars's core is probably solid.

Through a telescope on Earth, dark markings and an ice cap (bottom left) can be seen on Mars.

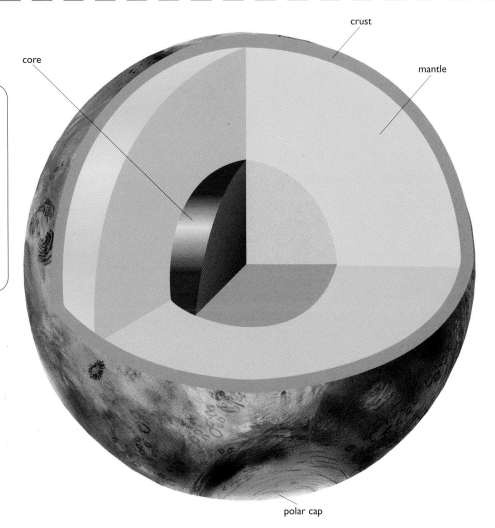

crust

core

mantle

polar cap

Like Earth, Mars is made up of layers. It has a hard outer crust and a mantle of heavier rock underneath. A solid iron core probably lies at Mars's center.

DAYS ON MARS

Like all the planets, Mars spins around, or rotates, on its axis as it travels in its orbit around the Sun. A planet's axis is an imaginary line running through it from its north pole to its south pole. Mars rotates once in about 24 hours and 37 minutes in Earth time. One complete rotation equals one day. This means that one day on Mars is just slightly longer than the 24-hour day we have on Earth. A Martian day is known as a sol. Astronomers have divided the sol into 24 Martian hours, so that each Martian hour lasts 61 Earth-minutes and 33 Earth-seconds.

MARS DATA

Diameter at equator:
4,220 miles (6,794 km)

Average distance from Sun:
142,000,000 miles
(228,000,000 km)

Rotates in: 24 hours, 37 minutes

Orbits Sun in: 687 days

Moons: 2

SEASONS ON MARS

As on Earth, the weather on Mars changes regularly over periods of time called seasons. The tilt of Mars's axis causes the planet to have seasons. Mars's axis tilts at an angle of 24 degrees, just a little more than Earth's axis. This tilt means that different parts of Mars lean toward or away from the Sun as the planet travels in its orbit. The part of the planet tilting toward the Sun receives more of the Sun's heat and grows warmer. When one half of the planet is tilted toward the Sun, the other half is tilted away. So when it is summer on Mars's northern half, it is winter on its southern half.

Above: On Mars, as on Earth, when one half of the planet is in daylight, the other half experiences darkness.

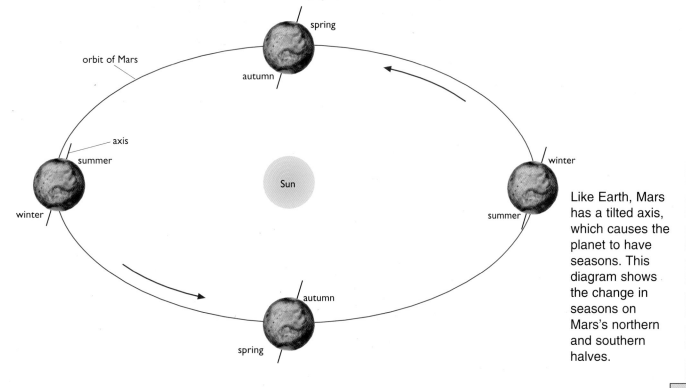

Like Earth, Mars has a tilted axis, which causes the planet to have seasons. This diagram shows the change in seasons on Mars's northern and southern halves.

THE MARTIAN MOONS

The American astronomer Asaph Hall discovered Mars's two moons in 1877. He named them Phobos and Deimos after the sons of the Roman god Mars. Both moons are small and have an irregular shape, sort of like a potato. Phobos, the larger moon, measures only about 17 miles (28 km) across at its widest point. Deimos is no more than 10 miles (16 km) across. Craters, or pits in the surface, cover both moons, and Phobos is marked with long grooves. Dusty soil and rocky boulders rest on each moon's surface.

Phobos orbits very close to Mars. In fact, it orbits closer to its planet than any other moon does. It travels at a distance of only about 3,700

Mars's two small moons, Phobos (above) and Deimos (right). Both have an irregular shape.

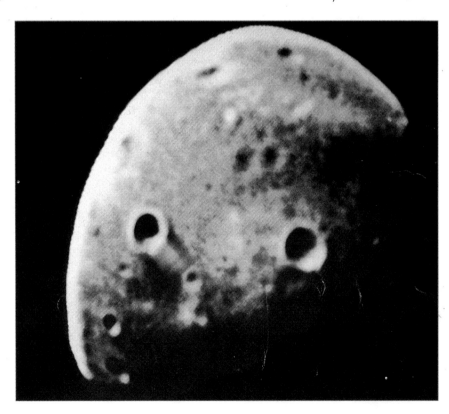

STAR POINT

In the 1960s, a Russian scientist named Iosif Shklovskii believed that Phobos was hollow. He thought it might be a huge space station built by intelligent Martians.

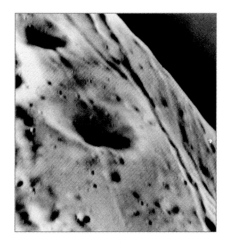

The surface of Phobos (top) is marked with long grooves and deep craters. Deimos's surface (bottom) is also covered with craters.

miles (6,000 km) from Mars. Because it is so close to Mars, Phobos speeds around the planet in less than eight hours, traveling from west to east. In comparison, Deimos takes over a day to orbit Mars. It orbits at a distance of about 12,000 miles (20,000 km) from the planet.

Astronomers think that Mars's potato-shaped moons may have once orbited the Sun as asteroids. Most of these rocky bodies travel around the Sun in what we call the asteroid belt, located between Mars and Jupiter. Phobos and Deimos would have been captured by Mars's gravity when they came close to the planet billions of years ago. Gravity is the attraction, or pull, one body has on the objects around it.

Phobos in orbit around Mars

This picture of Mars shows the icy south polar region. The large circular patch to the right is a great cloud of mist.

Atmosphere and Weather

The weather on Mars is always changing. There are swirling clouds, morning mists, blowing winds, and raging dust storms.

Compared to Earth, Mars has a very thin atmosphere. It is made up of about 95 percent carbon dioxide and small amounts of other gases, including nitrogen and argon. Mars's atmosphere

Highs and Lows

While temperatures vary widely across Mars, overall it is much colder than our home planet. Like Earth, Mars is warmest at the equator—an imaginary line around a planet, midway between its north and south poles. And also like Earth, Mars is coldest at its poles.

Temperatures on Mars vary from place to place, changing with the seasons. In the Martian summer, temperatures at the equator may rise to nearly 70°F (22°C). But elsewhere, daytime temperatures are generally below freezing. During the winter, temperatures may drop to less than –220°F (–140°C) at the poles. The average temperature on Mars is about –67°F (–55°C).

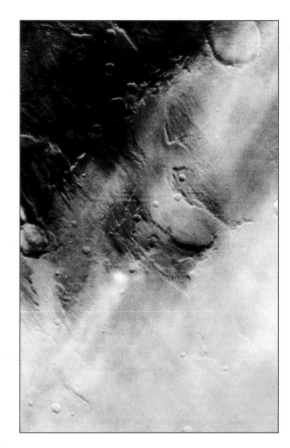

Above: Dust storms on Mars often begin on flat stretches of land like this one, called Solis Planium.

contains just a faint trace of oxygen—the gas that humans and animals on Earth must breathe to live.

Mars's atmosphere also contains small amounts of water vapor (water in its gas form). As on Earth, the water vapor forms clouds. Clouds on Mars swirl in the atmosphere and cluster around the higher slopes of mountains. Low clouds, or mist, also form in the valleys early in Mars's morning.

Martian Winds

Winds on Mars blow from the cold parts of the planet to the warmer parts. In general, Martian winds are light, but at times they can blow at speeds of up to 250 mph (400 km/h). These powerful winds whip up fine dust from Mars's surface to form dust storms in the atmosphere. Dust storms on Mars can last for weeks and cover the whole planet, with dust rising up to 15 miles (24 km) in the atmosphere.

Right: Winds on Mars stir up dust on its surface, leading to dust storms in the planet's thin atmosphere.

Mars's Landscape

High volcanoes, deep basins, long channels, and frozen polar caps are just some of the amazing features that cover Mars's surface.

Mars looks very different to the north and south of its equator. Ancient craters, or large pits in the surface, cover most of Mars's southern half. Astronomers believe that many of these craters are billions of years old. The surface of Mars's northern half is probably much younger. Unlike Mars's ancient cratered land, the landscape north of the equator is marked by plains, or flat stretches of land, that formed as recently as 1 billion years ago.

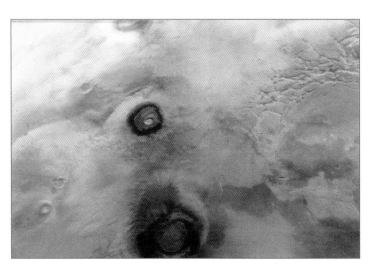

The Hubble Space Telescope orbits Earth at 380 miles (610 km) above our planet. It sends back pictures like this one of the Martian landscape. It observes the planet on a regular basis, following the changes that take place season by season.

THE MARTIAN VOLCANOES
Mars may be one of the smallest planets, but some of the largest volcanoes in the solar system rise on its northern half. Over millions of years, Mars's volcanoes erupted many times, pouring out floods of lava, or hot liquid rock. As the lava spread over Mars's surface, it cooled and hardened to form the planet's northern plains.

THE BIG FOUR
Mars's four largest volcanoes are not shaped like cones with steep sides, like many volcanoes on Earth. Instead, these volcanoes have a wide base and gently sloping sides. Similar volcanoes on Earth are called shield volcanoes. Three of Mars's largest volcanoes rise on a great bulge called Tharsis, near the planet's equator. The three volcanoes, named Ascraeus Mons, Pavonis Mons, and Arsia Mons, are strung out in a line. They are each about 9 miles (15 km) high and at least 250 miles (400 km) across at the base.

STAR POINT

Olympus Mons is 100 times the size of Earth's largest volcano, Mauna Loa, which is located in the Hawaiian Islands.

As big as they are, these three volcanoes are dwarfed by another volcano to the west called Olympus Mons. At its base, it measures nearly 400 miles (640 km) across. If Olympus Mons were on Earth, it would cover all of the state of Washington and nearly half of Oregon. The giant volcano rises to about 17 miles (27 km) above the surrounding landscape. That's three times the height of Mount Everest, the highest mountain on Earth.

VOLCANOES EVERYWHERE

To the north of the Tharsis Bulge sits another remarkable volcano called Alba Patera. It stands only a few miles high, but it spreads over an area as much as 400 miles (700 km) across. Also in the north is a grouping of three smaller volcanoes, in a region called Elysium.

A number of volcanoes lie near the huge crater called Hellas, on Mars's southern half. The volcanoes near this crater probably erupted when the crater formed as long as 4 billion years ago. In comparison, the four huge northern volcanoes may have erupted as recently as 1 billion years ago.

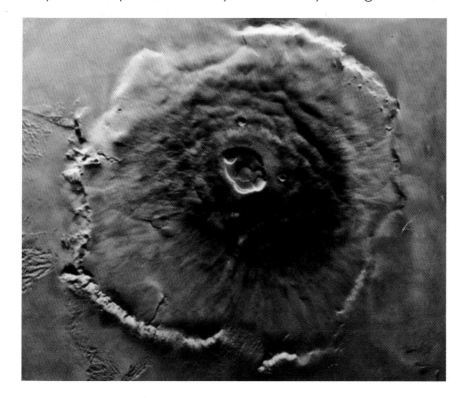

The giant volcano Olympus Mons (left) erupted time and time again, pouring out rivers of lava that flowed over Mars's surface. A model (below) shows what the volcano's crater would look like close up.

This image shows mainly the northern half of Mars. To the left are the three large volcanoes on the Tharsis Bulge. To their right is the great canyon system Valles Marineris.

CRATERS AND BASINS

Mars's southern half looks a lot like our Moon. Large and small craters cover the landscape. Astronomers believe that many of these craters formed about 4 billion years ago, when meteorites hit Mars's surface. Meteorites are rocky lumps from outer space that crash to the surface of another body, such as a planet or moon.

Blowing winds have eroded, or worn away, some of Mars's craters. Other craters have been flooded by lava from ancient volcanic eruptions. The craters vary in size from small pits to large ring structures more than 1,000 miles (1,600 km) across. The largest crater on Mars is the Hellas Basin, measuring as much as 1,200 miles (2,000 km) across.

A 3D view of part of Valles Marineris

MARS'S GRAND CANYON

An enormous canyon near Mars's equator stretches one-fourth of the way around the planet. It is often called the Grand Canyon of Mars, after Earth's famous canyon in Arizona. Its actual name is Valles Marineris. The canyon begins near the great Tharsis Bulge and runs east along the equator. Many branches fan out to the north and south of the main canyon.

With a length of about 2,500 miles (4,000 km), Valles Marineris is more than 10 times as long as the Grand Canyon on Earth. It is up to 120 miles (200 km) wide and as much as 4 miles (7 km) deep. In comparison, the Grand Canyon is at most only about 20 miles (30 km) wide and a little over 1 mile (1.6 km) deep.

The Difference

Valles Marineris and the Grand Canyon look similar, but they formed in very different ways. Earth's Grand Canyon was created by the Colorado River. Over hundreds of thousands of years, the river has slowly carved the Grand Canyon out of the rocks it flows over. In contrast, Valles Marineris was created over a much shorter period of time. It probably formed when a part of Mars's crust shifted and caused the surface to crack open.

The Grand Canyon, in Arizona

STAR POINT

Scientists have estimated that early in Mars's history, its surface may have been covered by 1,500 feet (465 m) of water.

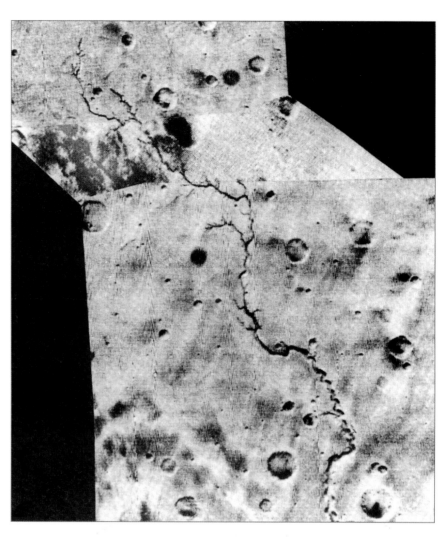

A channel zigzags across the surface of Mars for a distance of about 360 miles (575 km). It looks very similar to the channels that rivers make on Earth.

CHANNELS

A river did not carve out Valles Marineris, but there are signs elsewhere on Mars that water might have flooded the planet in the past. Winding channels run across different parts of Mars's surface. They appear to be places where rivers may once have flowed.

Some channels on Mars begin in high ground and gradually widen as they wind their way to lower ground, just as rivers on Earth widen as they flow downward. Other channels are not as wide and have smaller channels that branch off. In some channels, surface material has formed into patterns around obstacles such as craters. Astronomers believe that flowing water may have caused these patterns.

Water on Mars?

The Mars we know is a dry planet. But the existence of so many channels leads astronomers to believe that water may once have flooded the surface. Water might have spewed from erupting volcanoes billions of years ago, when Mars's inner layers were probably very hot. These volcanic eruptions would have also released huge amounts of different gases. Together, rising water vapor and other gases would have formed a thick atmosphere. A thicker atmosphere would have kept in more of the Sun's heat, so at one time the whole planet might have been much warmer.

Gradually the gases in Mars's thicker atmosphere would have drifted off into space. Most of the water vapor would have drifted off too, leaving only enough vapor in the planet's thin atmosphere to form clouds and freeze as ice caps at the poles. No liquid water remains on the planet, but water exists as ice in Mars's polar caps and may be frozen underneath the planet's dusty surface.

A deep valley cuts through the surface near Mars's equator and connects with the Amazon Plain (top). It is possible that this flat region was once the floor of a large ocean.

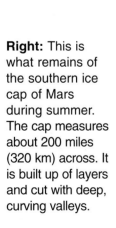

Above: Mars's northern polar cap has a noticeable spiral pattern, probably caused by swirling winds.

THE POLAR CAPS

For a long time, astronomers have noticed that the ice caps on Mars's north and south poles change in size. When they discovered that Mars has regular seasons, they realized that the polar caps grow and shrink as temperatures change. Both polar caps are biggest during winter, when more ice freezes, and smallest during summer, when more ice melts. Seasons in the north and south of the planet are opposite. This means that when one ice cap is at its largest, the other is at its smallest.

In winter at both poles, gas from Mars's atmosphere freezes on the ground, making the ice caps grow. These winter ice caps are probably made up of a mixture of frozen carbon dioxide and frozen water. When temperatures rise again in the summer, some of the ice turns into gas and goes back into the atmosphere. But it never gets warm enough at either pole to melt the ice caps entirely. The ice cap that remains at the north pole in summer is made up mainly of water ice, like the polar caps on Earth. The summer ice cap at the south pole is probably a mixture of water ice and frozen carbon dioxide.

Right: This is what remains of the southern ice cap of Mars during summer. The cap measures about 200 miles (320 km) across. It is built up of layers and cut with deep, curving valleys.

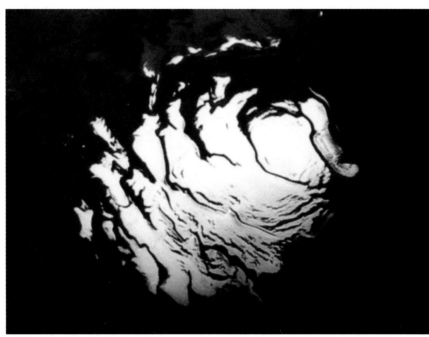

Mars Rocks

Rocks of all shapes and sizes are found on Mars's great plains, amid drifts and dunes of fine red soil.

Before we knew much about Mars's surface, astronomers expected the planet's flat northern plains to be like sandy deserts on Earth. Instead, astronomers discovered that thousands of rocks cover Mars's dusty plains. Martian rocks come in all shapes and sizes. Some are as small as pebbles, while others are as large as boulders. They can be rounded or sharp, dark or bright, pitted or smooth.

A VARIETY OF ROCKS

Where do all the rocks that cover the Martian soil come from? Some may have erupted from ancient volcanoes, which would have hurled rocks high into the sky while they poured out hot lava. Other rocks may have broken off from Mars's surface when meteorites struck the planet. Scientists also believe that flowing water on Mars may have deposited rocks on the surface. An example of this kind of rock lines the mouth of what is probably an ancient riverbed on Mars.

Large and small rocks cover much of Mars's rust-red surface, as seen on this plain called Chryse.

The Martian Soil

Dry, dusty soil covers everything on Mars's surface. Some of the soil is very fine, possibly as fine as talcum powder. It is blown by the wind into drifts or dunes that are similar to those in deserts on Earth. The Martian soil is rich in iron oxide, the substance that forms rust. The presence of iron oxide in the soil gives Mars its reddish color.

STAR POINT

The *Pathfinder* mission tested rocks on Mars by bombarding them with radiation. The way the rocks reflected the radiation helped scientists learn about their makeup.

TESTING THE ROCKS

In 1996, NASA (National Aeronautics and Space Administration) launched a probe called *Pathfinder*. It landed on Mars's surface in July 1997. Several different kinds of rock surrounded the area where *Pathfinder* landed. Most of the rocks appeared to have come from volcanic eruptions. Tests on the rocks showed that they were like two kinds of volcanic rock on Earth called basalt and andesite. *Pathfinder* craft also tested other rocks that looked like a rock called conglomerate found on Earth. This kind of rock forms in riverbeds.

Three different kinds of rocks are marked in this picture, taken by the *Pathfinder* probe. Red arrows point to rocks that are large and rounded and have a surface worn by the action of the weather. Blue arrows show small, gray angular rocks, while white arrows point to flat light-colored rocks.

Life on Mars?

People once believed that intelligent beings lived on Mars. We have since learned that Martians do not exist. But many scientists hope to find proof that some form of life did exist on Mars in the past.

In 1877, an Italian observer named Giovanni Schiaparelli studied Mars closely and reported seeing dark lines on the planet. He called them canals. Some people began to believe that intelligent beings had made these canals, or artificial waterways.

In 1894 the astronomer Percival Lowell set up an observatory at Flagstaff, Arizona, to study Mars. Like Schiaparelli, Lowell believed that he could see networks of canals on the Red Planet. Lowell wrote about the possibility of desperate Martians living on a planet that was slowly growing colder and drier. He believed that Martians had built canals to carry precious water from the melting ice caps to warmer areas near the equator. They needed the water, Lowell believed, to grow crops. But they were fighting a losing battle and were slowly dying out.

Other astronomers with equally good telescopes did not find any canals on Mars. They did not support the idea that intelligent Martians lived on the planet. But even in the early 1960s, many people thought that there might be some form of life on Mars.

This sketch of Mars, made by Percival Lowell, shows the canals that he believed he had seen on the planet. Lowell thought intelligent Martians had built these canals.

UNINVITED VISITORS

The English writer H. G. Wells took up this theme in his novel *The War of the Worlds* (1898). He wrote about a dying Martian race that could see how green and fertile Earth was. The Martians decided to send an army to Earth in

terrifying war machines so that they could invade and conquer their neighboring planet. This book gave more people the idea that intelligent beings might be living on Mars.

In 1938, the American actor Orson Welles produced a radio broadcast of a play based on *The War of the Worlds*. In the play, Martians were invading New Jersey. Thousands of American radio listeners did not realize they were hearing a play, and they panicked. Some people fled to their churches to pray, others locked themselves in their homes. Hundreds of terrified citizens called their local police. Frightened listeners eventually learned that Martians had not invaded Earth.

CLOSE-UP VIEWS

When space probes began visiting Mars in the late 1960s, astronomers learned that conditions on the planet are too harsh for life as we know it. The probes found no crops, no canals, and certainly no signs of intelligent Martians. However, if Mars was once warmer and had flowing water, life may have existed on the planet in the distant past. It is possible that we may one day find fossils, or the remains of living things, on Mars.

Above: This is a scene from the film of H. G. Wells's *The War of the Worlds*, which was first screened in 1953. It shows the tendril-like limb of a Martian reaching out for a terrified human.

Right: The probes that landed on Mars did not discover canals or intelligent Martians on the planet. Instead, they have shown that conditions on Mars are too harsh to support life.

METEORITE FROM MARS

In 1984, scientists discovered a meteorite in Antarctica that probably came from Mars around 16 million years ago. The chunk of Mars rock probably broke off from the planet when another meteorite slammed into it. The Mars meteorite, known as ALH84001, probably fell to Earth about 13,000 years ago. Some scientists believe the meteorite contains fossils of simple organisms, or life-forms, like the bacteria that live on Earth. This would mean that there has been life on Mars. Other scientists do not agree. They say that the tiny structures were created by a natural process on Earth and not by bacteria on Mars.

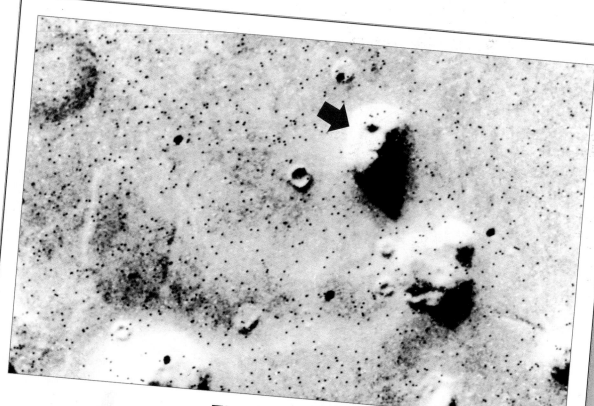

The Face on Mars

In 1976, a picture taken by a Viking probe showed what appeared to be a human-like face. Some people said that the face was carved by Martians. But in 1998, the *Mars Global Surveyor* showed that the face is just a natural rock formation on the planet's surface.

Above: This is what *Mariner 4* would have looked like as it approached Mars in July 1965.

Missions to Mars

Since 1965, several space probes have visited the Red Planet, sending back pictures of giant volcanoes, misty valleys, wind-blown deserts, and wide craters.

The Soviet Union tried to launch the first space probe to Mars in 1960. Over the next few years, they attempted to launch more probes, but none of them reached the planet. NASA also had problems with its first probe to Mars, *Mariner 3*, which was launched in November 1964 and never made it to Mars.

Also launched in November 1964, NASA's *Mariner 4* became the first space probe to reach Mars. It flew past the planet on July 14, 1965, at a distance of less than 6,000 miles (10,000 km). *Mariner 4* sent back information about Mars's atmosphere and took pictures that showed craters on the planet's surface. These craters looked much like the craters on the Moon.

Two more probes, *Mariner 6* and *Mariner 7*, reached Mars in July and August of 1969, coming within 2,200 miles (3,500 km) of the planet. Together, *Mariner 6* and *Mariner 7* sent back nearly 200 pictures. They showed

Left: *Mariner 6* revealed the surface of Mars clearly for the first time. It showed that parts of the planet look much like the Moon.

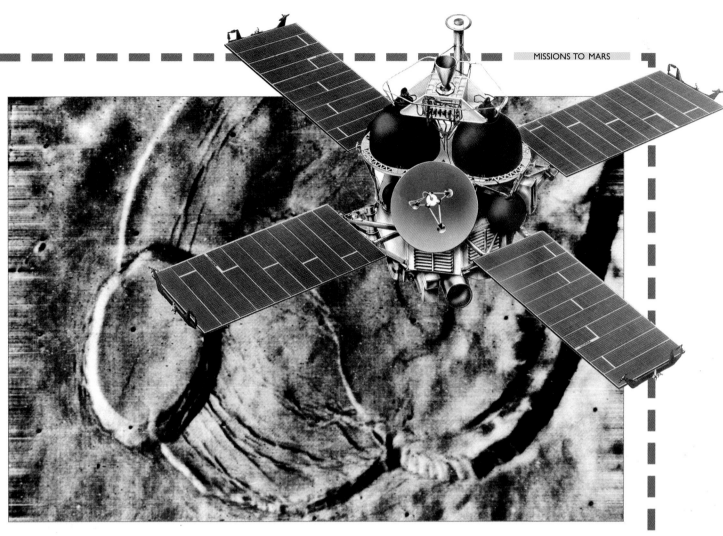

Mariner 9 took this picture of the mouth of Mars's largest volcano, Olympus Mons.

that Mars had desert-like plains, and many craters. They also photographed the southern polar cap and recorded temperatures as low as −190°F (−125°C).

MARINER 9 IN ORBIT

The next probe to reach Mars, *Mariner 9*, went into orbit around the planet in November 1971. At the time, Mars was in the grip of a dust storm, which prevented *Mariner 9* from revealing much of the planet's surface.

Within days of the Martian skies clearing, *Mariner 9* spotted two of Mars's outstanding natural features—its remarkable Valles Marineris and the massive ancient volcano, Olympus Mons. By the time *Mariner 9* ran out of fuel, in October 1972, it had sent back more than 7,000 pictures and photographed almost the entire planet. During this time, several Soviet spacecraft had also begun to successfully explore Mars.

THE VIKING INVASION

Mariner 9 paved the way for an exciting mission called *Viking*. On this mission, two identical probes were sent to Mars. NASA planned for the probes to release landers—spacecraft that would drop down to Mars and explore its surface.

Viking 1 sped into space in late August 1975, with *Viking 2* following in early September. For more than 10 months, the *Viking* spacecraft cruised through space. *Viking 1* went into orbit around Mars in June 1976, followed by *Viking 2* a few weeks later. In their orbits, the *Viking* probes came as close as 950 miles (1,500 km) to Mars's surface to photograph possible places for the landers to drop.

The *Viking* landers descend to Mars's surface. The landing capsule separates from the *Viking* orbiter (1). The capsule maneuvers so that its heat shield faces forward (2). A parachute slows it down (3) before the lander separates and uses rockets to brake (4), so that it lands gently (5). The orbiter stays in orbit (6).

TOUCHDOWN

The *Viking* orbiters released their landing craft to chosen sites in July and September. The *Viking 1* lander touched down on a flat plains region known as Chryse, and the *Viking 2* lander touched down hundreds of miles away on another part of Mars called Utopia. Surprisingly, the landers' cameras showed that the landscape of both areas looked almost the same.

The landers took pictures, reported on the Martian weather, and dug into the soil. A scoop on each lander's digging arm placed soil samples into a miniature laboratory, where experiments were carried out on them. The experiments tested the soil for traces of life. But no traces were found.

Meanwhile, the *Viking* orbiters were photographing the planet, sending back the most detailed views of Mars to date. Together, they took more than 51,000 pictures. The final transmissions from the *Viking* mission were sent in November 1982, when scientists lost contact with the spacecraft.

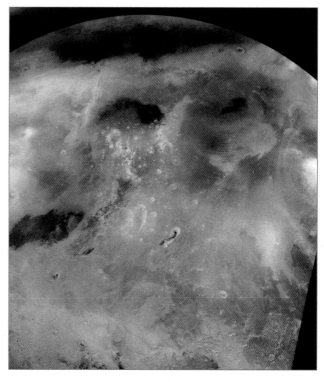

Above: This photograph taken by a *Viking* orbiter shows the red soil on Mars's surface and white clouds in its thin atmosphere.

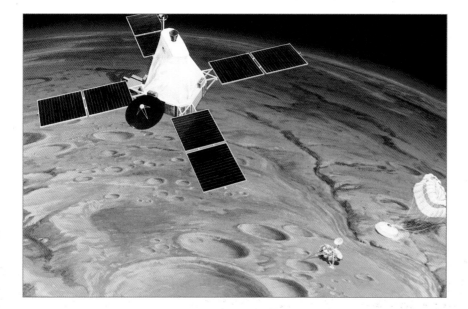

Left: The *Viking* orbiters measured about 32 feet (9.8 meters) across the paddle-like solar panels. Each had two cameras, which were like the TV cameras used in broadcasting. They took pictures through a series of colored filters so that color pictures could be created. Other instruments measured temperatures and the amount of water vapor in the atmosphere.

Above: As the rover *Sojourner* explored the Martian surface, it transmitted its findings to *Pathfinder*, which relayed them back to Earth.

Right: *Pathfinder* and *Sojourner* on Mars. In the background are the mountains known as the Twin Peaks.

THE MARTIAN ROVER

NASA did not send another probe to Mars for nearly 15 years. In July 1997, *Pathfinder* landed on Mars's surface. After *Pathfinder* landed, it unfolded a set of petal-like solar panels. The panels collected sunlight and used it to power its instruments. *Pathfinder*'s first photographs showed distant mountains, the rim of a crater, and a reddish surface scattered with rocks. The landscape looked very similar to the areas that the *Viking* probes had observed.

But *Pathfinder* carried more than cameras. It carried a wheeled rover called *Sojourner*, which traveled slowly over the Martian surface. This small vehicle inspected nearby rocks and analyzed their makeup. *Pathfinder* and *Sojourner* sent back data for nearly three months.

By this time, another NASA spacecraft called *Mars Global Surveyor* was orbiting Mars. It sent back highly detailed pictures of the surface from space. Then in late 1998 and early 1999 the *Climate Orbiter* and the *Polar Lander* launched from Earth. Scientists continue to learn more and more about our mysterious neighbor. Someday, perhaps we will learn whether life has ever existed on the Red Planet.

Glossary

asteroid: a small rocky body that circle the Sun or another heavenly body

atmosphere: the layer of gases around a planet or other heavenly body

axis: an imaginary line through a planet from its north to its south poles

basin: a large crater on a planet's surface, often formed by a meteorite impact

canal: artificial waterway

core: the center part of a planet or moon

crater: a pit on the surface of a planet or a moon

crust: the hard outer layer of a rocky planet like Earth or Mars

erode: to gradually wear away the surface of a planet or other body

equator: an imaginary line around a planet, midway between its north and south poles

fossil: the remains of living things

gravity: the attraction, or pull, that every heavenly body has on objects on or near it

lava: hot liquid rock that erupts from volcanoes, cools, and hardens

mantle: a layer of rock underneath the crust of a rocky planet

meteorite: a lump of rock or metal from space that falls to the surface of a planet or a moon

orbit: the path in space of one heavenly body around another, such as Mars around the Sun

orbiter: a space probe that circles in orbit around a planet or moon

plain: a flat stretch of land

planet: a large body that circles in space around the Sun.

polar cap: a region near the north and south poles on Mars and earth that is covered with ice

probe: a spacecraft that travels from Earth to explore bodies in the solar system

rover: a wheeled vehicle that explores the surface of a planet

shield volcano: a volcano with a wide base and gently sloping sides

sol: a Martian day

solar system: the Sun and all the bodies that circle around it

terrestrial: like Earth

volcano: a place where hot liquid rock from underground forces its way to the surface of a planet or moon

water vapor: water in the form of gas

Index